Beyond Service:

Next-Level Leadership

for a

Conscious World

Zen Benefiel, ma, mba, tlc

Be The Dream Publishing ©2024

ISBN: 9798341315020

Contents

Introduction:
　Evolving Leadership for a Conscious World i

Chapter 1:
　Rethinking Sustainability – From Sustaining to Regenerating 1

Chapter 2:
　Leadership in Harmony with Nature 5

Chapter 3:
　The Art of Conscious Listening 11

Chapter 4:
　Co-Creation and Collective Wisdom 15

Chapter 5:
　Viewing Organizations as Ecosystems 21

Chapter 6:
　The Ripple Effect of Decisions 25

Chapter 7:
　Cultivating Self-Awareness and Autonomy 33

Chapter 8:
　Coaching for Purpose and Potential 37

Chapter 9:
　Distributed Decision-Making 45

Chapter 10:
　Embracing Diversity, Equity, and Inclusion 49

Chapter 11:
  The Practice of Mindfulness in Leadership 55

Chapter 12:
  Leadership in Action 59

Chapter 13:
  Discovering Organizational Purpose 65

Chapter 14:
  Inspiring Others with a Purpose-Driven Mission 69

Chapter 15:
  Seeing the Big Picture in Quantum Leadership 77

Chapter 16:
  Leading with Agility and Embracing the Unknown 81

Chapter 17:
  Building Trust Through Emotional Resonance 87

Chapter 18:
  Fostering a Positive Organizational Culture 91

Conclusion:
  The Journey to Next-Level Leadership 97

About the Author 101

Introduction:
Evolving Leadership for a Conscious World

The world is changing, and so is our understanding of leadership. As we face unprecedented challenges in business, social structures, and environmental stability, a new kind of leadership is emerging—one that is attuned not only to serving others but to regenerating systems, fostering deep connections, and operating with an awareness of the bigger picture. Traditional models of leadership, including servant leadership, have laid a strong foundation by emphasizing compassion, service, and humility. However, as our world becomes more interconnected and our challenges more complex, a need for "next-level leadership" has surfaced—leadership that is deeply conscious, regenerative, and responsive.

This book, *Beyond Service: Next-Level Leadership for a Conscious World,* explores this evolution, integrating insights from regenerative thinking, systems theory, and quantum science with practices like mindfulness and emotional resonance. It builds on the principles of servant leadership and extends them to encompass new concepts such as conscious collaboration, distributed decision-making, and sustainable impact. These principles recognize the essential interconnectedness of people, organizations, and the planet. Here, leadership is not just about guiding others but about engaging with purpose, inspiring through example, and fostering a shared sense of responsibility.

Why Next-Level Leadership?

At the heart of next-level leadership is the understanding that every decision we make ripples beyond our organizations, affecting communities and ecosystems around the globe. Leaders today face questions that go beyond the bottom line. How can we create environments that inspire people to bring their full, authentic selves to their work? What role can organizations play in healing and restoring our planet? And, crucially, how can leaders adapt and respond to uncertainty with resilience and grace?

By expanding upon traditional servant leadership, next-level leadership addresses these questions by advocating for practices that regenerate the planet, empower individuals, and foster collaboration across boundaries. Leaders are called not just to serve but to transform—to view their role as both custodians of the present and architects of the future.

What You Will Find in This Book

In *Beyond Service,* we invite you to explore new dimensions of leadership, structured around nine core concepts. Each chapter provides practical insights, real-world examples, and reflective exercises to help you deepen your understanding and develop as a conscious, purpose-driven leader. You will learn about:

- **Regenerative Leadership**, which encourages leaders to restore and revitalize the systems they touch, creating a positive impact that extends beyond sustainability.

- **Conscious Collaboration**, where trust and deep listening become the foundation for collective wisdom and innovative solutions.

- **Systems Thinking**, helping you to see your organization as a complex ecosystem where every decision has far-reaching effects.

- **Transformational Empowerment**, a way to inspire others to discover their purpose and unleash their full potential.

- And much more, including mindful leadership, quantum adaptability, and resonant culture-building.

A Call to Conscious Action

This book is not just a guide; it's a call to action. Leadership today requires courage, adaptability, and a willingness to venture into uncharted territory. As we explore each principle together, remember that the true measure of leadership is not in what we accomplish alone but in how we uplift, empower, and connect with those around us.

In embarking on this journey toward next-level leadership, you are not simply transforming your organization—you are contributing to the conscious evolution of our world. Let us lead with purpose, inspire through compassion, and, together, create a legacy of positive change for generations to come.

Part 1:

Regenerative Leadership

Creating Lasting Impact

Chapter 1:
Rethinking Sustainability – From Sustaining to Regenerating

"Sustainability asks us to maintain; regeneration invites us to revitalize and renew."

As the challenges of climate change, resource depletion, and ecological degradation intensify, the concept of sustainability—long considered the gold standard of responsible leadership—has come under a new lens. While sustainability seeks to minimize harm, regenerative leadership goes a step further, asking leaders to become catalysts for active renewal, restoration, and revitalization. In this chapter, we examine the evolution from sustainable practices to regenerative ones and why the shift is critical for a future that supports life in all its forms.

The Limitations of Sustainability

- **Beyond "Do No Harm"**: Sustainability often centers around minimizing negative impacts. But, in practice, this approach can fall short in addressing the full spectrum of our environmental, social, and economic challenges.

- **Renewal as a Responsibility**: Regenerative leadership calls for leaders to see their role as stewards of ecosystems, ensuring that each action and decision contributes to the active regeneration of the resources, communities, and environments they engage with.

Principles of Regenerative Leadership

- **Active Stewardship**: Regenerative leaders focus on nourishing resources rather than merely preserving them. This principle prioritizes actions that improve environmental health and support social well-being, often extending beyond traditional business objectives.

- **Circular Design Thinking**: Adopting circularity in products, processes, and structures encourages waste reduction, resource efficiency, and continuous renewal. Leaders who use circular design prioritize the lifecycle of products and services, envisioning how materials can be repurposed, recycled, and reintegrated.

Real-World Examples of Regenerative Leadership in Action

- Highlight companies and leaders transforming industries by rethinking their supply chains, adopting regenerative agriculture, and implementing circular economy practices.

- Explore case studies that illustrate how these leaders go beyond sustainability, impacting ecosystems, communities, and even employee well-being through regenerative initiatives.

Example: Interface's Mission Zero and Climate Take Back Initiatives

Interface, a global flooring company, set a bold goal called "Mission Zero," aiming to eliminate any negative environmental impact by 2020. Through sustainable innovations in its production processes, it reduced greenhouse gas emissions and water usage.

Building on its success, Interface launched the "Climate Take Back" initiative, aiming to reverse global warming by designing carbon-negative products and supporting renewable energy. Interface's journey demonstrates how regenerative leadership transforms business practices into powerful climate solutions.

Case Study: Patagonia's Commitment to Regenerative Agriculture

Patagonia, known for its environmental commitment, has pioneered regenerative agriculture through its supply chain by sourcing materials from regenerative farms. The company supports regenerative organic certification, which ensures that its cotton, wool, and food products restore soil health, biodiversity, and carbon capture. This approach not only minimizes environmental harm but actively contributes to soil regeneration, illustrating a shift from sustainability to regeneration.

Practical Steps for Becoming a Regenerative Leader

1. **Evaluate the Lifecycle of Decisions**: Encourage a systems-thinking approach where every decision is evaluated for its short- and long-term impact on natural and human ecosystems.

2. **Integrate Regenerative Goals into Strategic Planning**: Set specific, measurable objectives related to environmental health, social responsibility, and economic resilience.

3. **Engage in Dialogue with Environmental and Social Experts**: Collaborate with environmental scientists, social advocates, and community leaders to shape initiatives that contribute positively to the environment and society.

By embracing a regenerative mindset, leaders cultivate an organization that doesn't just function sustainably but actively contributes to a thriving world. This transition marks a pivotal shift from the mindset of preservation to one of contribution, where the role of a leader is to uplift, renew, and restore.

Chapter 2:
Leadership in Harmony with Nature

"To lead effectively, we must be in harmony with the cycles, rhythms, and wisdom of the natural world."

Regenerative leadership requires a relationship with nature that goes beyond conventional environmental concerns. At its core, it's about recognizing and working within nature's rhythms, cycles, and principles. This chapter explores how leaders can deepen their connection with the natural world, embracing its intelligence as a model for resilience, adaptation, and renewal.

Learning from Nature's Wisdom

- **Embracing Cyclical Processes**: Nature operates in cycles—birth, growth, death, and renewal. By embracing these cycles, leaders learn to anticipate periods of growth and renewal, as well as times of rest and reflection.

- **Adaptation and Resilience**: In nature, adaptability and resilience are survival mechanisms. Leaders who internalize these values cultivate agile, resilient organizations that can navigate change and crisis with greater ease.

- **Diversity as Strength**: Ecosystems thrive on diversity, where different species contribute unique strengths to the whole. Similarly, leaders who value diversity foster workplaces rich in perspective, skill, and creativity.

Nature-Inspired Decision-Making Frameworks

- **Biomimicry in Leadership**: Biomimicry encourages looking to nature for solutions to complex problems. Leaders who adopt biomimetic thinking apply principles like self-sustenance, efficiency, and symbiosis to design processes, products, and systems that work in harmony with natural forces.

- **Permaculture Principles**: Permaculture is an agricultural approach centered on sustainable and self-sufficient ecosystems. Leaders can apply permaculture's "observe and interact" principle, ensuring that decisions respect the ecosystems they impact and that people and resources thrive in balance.

Case Studies of Nature-Harmonized Leadership

- Explore examples of companies and leaders who integrate nature-based approaches, from permaculture in community initiatives to biomimetic product design.

- Highlight organizations that embed natural rhythms into work culture, like flexible schedules that mirror seasonal cycles or workspace designs that mimic natural environments.

Example: Google's "The Biophilic Office" in Mountain View

Google's headquarters in Mountain View, California, incorporates biophilic design elements, like natural lighting, ventilation, and indoor plants, which emulate the feel of natural environments. Studies within Google show that these design elements enhance employee well-being, creativity, and productivity. By aligning workspace design with natural principles, Google sets a model for how leaders can use nature-inspired environments to support employee satisfaction and engagement.

Case Study: Biomimicry in the Designs of Janine Benyus

Biologist and innovation consultant Janine Benyus, co-founder of the Biomimicry Institute, helps companies design products inspired by nature. For example, by studying how nature repels water, Benyus and her team developed self-cleaning surfaces for buildings and products, reducing the need for harsh chemicals. Benyus's work exemplifies how leaders can apply principles from nature to create sustainable innovations in their fields.

Practices for Leaders to Cultivate Harmony with Nature

1. **Spend Time in Natural Environments**: Regularly connect with nature, not only to recharge but to observe and learn. Leaders who spend time in natural settings often find inspiration for managing complex challenges and fostering patience, adaptability, and humility.

2. **Engage in Ecological Training or Workshops**: Workshops in biomimicry, regenerative agriculture, or permaculture can provide leaders with practical tools for integrating nature's wisdom into their work.

3. **Champion Environmentally Aligned Policies**: Advocate for workplace practices that protect and regenerate natural systems, from waste reduction initiatives to energy conservation measures.

Reflection and Action Points

- How can you introduce natural rhythms and processes into your organization?

- In what ways can your organization adapt its policies to actively support environmental health?

- What new insights have you gained from observing nature, and how can these inform your leadership approach?

Closing Thoughts on Part 1: Embracing Regeneration and Harmony

Regenerative leadership is not just about environmental sustainability; it's about fostering a mindset that revitalizes people, processes, and the planet. By drawing inspiration from nature's resilience and embracing regenerative practices, leaders can become not just stewards of resources but champions of lasting, harmonious impact.

Part 2:

Conscious Collaboration

Building Transformative Teams

Chapter 3:
The Art of Conscious Listening

"True collaboration begins with a simple yet profound act: the willingness to listen without an agenda."

One of the most underestimated tools in conscious collaboration is the art of listening—not just hearing words, but truly understanding the perspectives, emotions, and motivations of others. Conscious listening involves a deep commitment to being fully present, setting aside preconceived judgments, and tuning into what each person brings to the table. In this chapter, we explore how listening deeply enhances teamwork, builds trust, and creates a foundation for authentic collaboration.

What is Conscious Listening?

- **Presence and Focus**: Conscious listening requires being fully present in each interaction, avoiding distractions, and focusing on the speaker without formulating responses. It's about valuing the conversation and the person fully.

- **Suspending Judgment**: In conscious listening, leaders practice openness by setting aside personal biases and assumptions, allowing them to connect with others on a deeper level and foster mutual understanding.

- **Seeking to Understand, Not Respond**: Leaders often feel the urge to respond or solve problems immediately. Conscious listening encourages them to first seek understanding, creating a safe space for others to voice thoughts and feelings fully.

Why Conscious Listening Matters in Leadership

- **Building Trust and Psychological Safety**: When team members feel truly heard, trust flourishes. They're more likely to share innovative ideas, express concerns, and take risks in a psychologically safe environment.

- **Enhancing Collective Intelligence**: Conscious listening brings more perspectives to the surface, enhancing collective intelligence and leading to richer solutions.

- **Reducing Miscommunication and Conflict**: Many workplace conflicts stem from misunderstandings. Conscious listening minimizes these issues by ensuring each person feels understood and valued.

Practices for Developing Conscious Listening

1. **Active Listening Exercises**: Regularly practice summarizing, paraphrasing, and clarifying what the speaker is saying, showing that you are engaged and open to their viewpoint.

2. **Mindfulness Techniques**: Engage in mindfulness practices that enhance focus and presence, helping to reduce distractions during interactions.

3. **Reflective Listening Sessions**: Set up sessions where team members can practice reflective listening, focusing solely on each other's perspectives without interruption or judgment.

Real-World Applications of Conscious Listening

- **Case Studies of Teams Built on Listening Culture**: Stories of organizations that have fostered transformative team dynamics by making conscious listening a core value.

- **Examples of Leaders Who Prioritize Listening**: Highlight leaders who have successfully resolved conflicts, strengthened their teams, and enhanced collaboration through focused listening practices.

By developing conscious listening, leaders build teams where people feel respected, understood, and motivated to contribute their best. This foundation of trust is essential for creating an environment where collaboration can thrive.

Example: IBM's Open Collaboration for Product Development

IBM embraced open collaboration by launching a digital platform where employees, customers, and partners can contribute to product innovation. Through active listening and feedback loops, IBM adapts products according to real-time user insights. This inclusive approach boosts trust, fosters innovation, and aligns the company's products with user needs, illustrating the power of conscious listening in collaborative development.

Case Study: Pixar's "Braintrust" Feedback Sessions

Pixar's "Braintrust" sessions are a great example of conscious listening in action. During these sessions, directors and producers present their projects to a group of peers, who give candid feedback. Braintrust attendees listen carefully to understand each project's vision, providing feedback that empowers the creator rather than imposing directives. This approach creates an atmosphere of trust and collaborative improvement, allowing directors to feel both supported and creatively challenged.

Chapter 4:
Co-Creation and Collective Wisdom

"In true co-creation, leaders become facilitators of shared vision and purpose, bringing together diverse minds to solve complex challenges."

Once the foundation of conscious listening is laid, leaders can elevate collaboration to the level of co-creation. Co-creation goes beyond traditional collaboration by inviting all team members to contribute to a shared vision, drawing on their collective wisdom to innovate, problem-solve, and grow. In this chapter, we explore the principles and practices of co-creation, emphasizing how leaders can guide teams toward realizing transformative outcomes together.

The Principles of Co-Creation

- **Shared Ownership**: In co-creation, every team member has a stake in the process and outcome, which increases commitment, accountability, and satisfaction.

- **Harnessing Collective Wisdom**: Co-creation leverages the knowledge, experiences, and creativity of all team members, often resulting in solutions far richer than any one person could achieve alone.

- **Flexibility and Adaptability**: Unlike rigid top-down decision-making, co-creation allows for flexibility, adapting as ideas evolve and feedback is integrated, leading to organic, innovative solutions.

Steps to Build a Co-Creative Team Culture

1. **Define a Shared Vision and Values**: Begin by working with the team to develop a common purpose and core values that

guide the co-creative process. When everyone is aligned with a vision, collective efforts have a stronger foundation.

2. **Encourage Openness and Diversity of Thought**: Embrace cognitive diversity, inviting different perspectives, experiences, and ideas. Encourage everyone to voice unique viewpoints without fear of judgment or reprisal.

3. **Facilitate Open-Ended Brainstorming Sessions**: Hold sessions where team members can brainstorm freely, focusing on generating ideas rather than evaluating them prematurely. Leaders act as facilitators, guiding the flow without dominating it.

Challenges and Solutions in Co-Creation

- **Balancing Structure and Freedom**: While co-creation thrives on openness, it also needs structure. Leaders can provide a framework that allows creative freedom while maintaining focus on goals.

- **Navigating Conflicts**: Co-creation may surface diverse opinions, sometimes leading to tension. Leaders can use conscious listening to mediate and facilitate discussions that turn conflicts into constructive learning experiences.

Real-World Examples of Co-Creative Leadership

- **Case Study of a Co-Created Project**: An example of an organization that successfully used co-creation to innovate and solve a significant challenge.

- **Leaders as Facilitators of Collective Vision**: Stories of leaders who excel in guiding teams toward a shared vision by focusing on co-creation and inclusivity.

Example: IKEA's Collaboration with Customers for Sustainable Living Solutions

IKEA collaborates with customers to co-create eco-friendly solutions through its "Better Living" initiative. This digital platform invites customers to share sustainable practices and challenges, like reducing waste or conserving energy. IKEA collects insights and ideas from these interactions, which are then used to refine its product lines and develop new, sustainable household solutions.

For instance, IKEA launched sustainable products, such as energy-efficient LED lights and water-saving faucets, directly inspired by customer feedback. By inviting customers to be part of the solution, IKEA fosters a culture of co-creation that empowers individuals to contribute to sustainability while aligning its business with eco-friendly practices.

Case Study: LEGO's Collaborative Innovation with Fans

LEGO's online "Ideas" platform allows fans to submit new product concepts. If a design gets enough votes, it is reviewed for production, and the creator is rewarded. This model of co-creation invites LEGO's audience to shape the brand's product line, fostering a strong sense of community and driving sales. Through co-creation, LEGO harnesses the creative power of its customers, showing how collective wisdom drives engagement and innovation.

Practical Tools for Leaders to Cultivate Co-Creation

- **Collective Intelligence Platforms**: Introduce digital tools that facilitate idea-sharing, such as crowdsourcing platforms and team brainstorming apps.

- **Rotating Leadership Roles**: Encourage rotating roles in meetings or projects, giving team members the chance to lead and contribute from different perspectives.

- **Reflection and Feedback Sessions**: Hold regular sessions for feedback, allowing the team to refine the co-creation process and address any challenges.

Reflection and Action Points

- What steps can you take to foster a stronger sense of ownership and co-creation within your team?

- How can you integrate diverse perspectives into your decision-making processes?

- In what ways can you act as a facilitator, empowering your team to draw on their collective wisdom?

Closing Thoughts on Part 2: Cultivating Conscious Collaboration

Conscious collaboration is more than teamwork; it is an intentional practice of listening, understanding, and co-creating that amplifies the collective strength of individuals. By developing conscious listening and fostering a culture of co-creation, leaders become facilitators of innovation, trust, and shared success. As we evolve our leadership styles, these practices become essential tools in guiding teams to create transformative results that benefit individuals, organizations, and communities alike.

Part 3:

Systems Thinking in Leadership

Navigating Complexity

Chapter 5:
Viewing Organizations as Ecosystems

"Leadership is not only about guiding people but about understanding how each part of an organization connects, influences, and contributes to the whole."

In our interconnected world, organizations cannot afford to operate in silos. Systems thinking offers a lens through which leaders can view their organizations as complex ecosystems, where every element is interdependent and influences the health and success of the whole. This chapter explores how adopting an ecosystem perspective can help leaders make more informed, resilient, and sustainable decisions.

What is Systems Thinking?

- **The Big Picture Approach**: Systems thinking involves looking beyond isolated actions and focusing on how various parts of an organization—departments, individuals, and processes—are interconnected.

- **Feedback Loops and Interdependence**: By understanding feedback loops (how actions create reactions that return to influence the original source), leaders gain insight into how decisions can have cascading effects across the organization.

- **Holistic Decision-Making**: Leaders who apply systems thinking make decisions that account for short- and long-term impacts, as well as effects on diverse stakeholders, including employees, customers, communities, and the environment.

Benefits of Viewing Organizations as Ecosystems

- **Improved Adaptability and Resilience**: Ecosystems thrive through adaptability. Organizations that embrace systems thinking can better anticipate change and respond to crises.

- **Enhanced Collaboration and Reduced Silos**: Viewing the organization as an ecosystem encourages departments to see how they impact each other, fostering greater collaboration and breaking down silos.

- **Sustainable Success**: Systems thinking shifts the focus from immediate gains to long-term sustainability, enabling leaders to build organizations that prioritize ethical practices and consider their broader impact on society.

Building a Systems Thinking Mindset

1. **Map Out Organizational Relationships**: Leaders can create visual maps to show connections and dependencies among departments, teams, and processes, highlighting how each part contributes to the overall ecosystem.

2. **Embrace a "Cause and Effect" Mindset**: Encourage leaders and team members to consider how their actions might ripple through the organization and beyond. This mindset shift encourages responsible, informed decision-making.

3. **Encourage Cross-Functional Collaboration**: Systems thinking flourishes in environments where cross-departmental collaboration is prioritized. Leaders can promote this by facilitating regular interdepartmental meetings, workshops, and project teams.

Real-World Applications of Systems Thinking in Organizations

- **Case Studies of Ecosystem-Oriented Companies**: Examples of organizations that have adopted systems thinking to foster innovation, address challenges, and drive sustainable change.

- **Leaders who Champion Systems Thinking**: Profiles of leaders who successfully navigate complexity through systems thinking, and how it has enabled them to create interconnected, resilient organizations.

Example: The Global Impact of IKEA's Circularity Approach

IKEA's commitment to circularity reflects systems thinking, focusing on the lifecycle of products from design to disposal. By offering "buy-back" programs and promoting second-life options for furniture, IKEA's system encourages customers to recycle products, reducing waste. This ecosystem approach involves both IKEA and its customers, demonstrating how systems thinking can reduce environmental impact through holistic engagement.

Case Study: Whole Foods Market's Decentralized Ecosystem Model

Whole Foods operates on a decentralized model where individual store teams make decisions tailored to their local communities. By giving stores autonomy, Whole Foods creates an interconnected ecosystem where each location serves its unique customer base while contributing to the company's overall mission of sustainability and community health. This decentralized structure encourages adaptability and meets local demands effectively.

Reflection and Action Points

- What are the interdependencies in your organization that could benefit from more intentional alignment?
- How might systems thinking change the way you approach challenges or opportunities?
- In what ways can you foster a mindset shift in your team to embrace an ecosystem perspective?

By developing a systems thinking approach, leaders not only strengthen their organizations but also build structures that can adapt, evolve, and positively impact the larger systems—communities, markets, and ecosystems—they operate within.

Chapter 6:
The Ripple Effect of Decisions

"Every decision sends waves through the organization, affecting people, processes, and outcomes in ways often unseen by those making the choice."

In a systems-oriented organization, decisions cannot be isolated events. Every choice has a ripple effect, sending waves through different levels and influencing outcomes that can extend far beyond the initial intent. In this chapter, we dive into the complexities of decision-making in systems thinking, helping leaders understand and manage the broader consequences of their actions.

Understanding the Ripple Effect

- **Seeing Beyond Immediate Outcomes**: Leaders often focus on the primary impact of decisions. Systems thinking encourages consideration of secondary and tertiary impacts—how the decision will affect teams, partners, customers, and long-term goals.

- **Anticipating Unintended Consequences**: Even well-intentioned decisions can have unforeseen impacts. By examining potential outcomes from multiple angles, leaders can identify and mitigate unintended consequences.

- **Influencing Organizational Culture and Morale**: Decisions can send powerful signals to the organization about values and priorities. Leaders who understand this ripple effect can make choices that strengthen culture, boost morale, and reinforce trust.

Steps for Making Decisions with Systems Thinking

1. **Consider Stakeholder Impact**: Before making decisions, leaders can examine how each option affects key stakeholders, including employees, customers, and the community. This encourages a broader and more inclusive decision-making process.

2. **Assess Short-Term vs. Long-Term Impacts**: Systems thinking promotes a balance between immediate gains and sustainable outcomes. Leaders can evaluate how decisions align with both current and future goals.

3. **Use Scenario Planning and "What If" Exercises**: Leaders can work with their teams to envision different scenarios for each decision, exploring potential ripple effects to anticipate challenges and maximize positive impact.

Case Studies on Ripple Effect in Decision-Making

- **Example of Companies Navigating Complex Decisions**: Stories of organizations that have successfully applied systems thinking to complex decisions, considering their ripple effects on culture, employee engagement, and community impact.

- **Leaders as Ripple Effect Role Models**: Profiles of leaders who practice conscientious decision-making, illustrating how they account for ripple effects and inspire similar awareness in their teams.

Example: Levi's Commitment to Water Reduction

Levi Strauss & Co. launched its "Water<Less" initiative to reduce water usage in its denim manufacturing process. This decision

significantly cut down water consumption, saving over 3 billion liters by using innovative techniques. Beyond Levi's internal practices, this initiative inspired suppliers and even competitors to adopt similar water-saving technologies.

Levi's ripple effect didn't stop at its supply chain; it extended to consumers through educational campaigns, encouraging customers to wash jeans less frequently and use cold water to reduce environmental impact. This example shows how one company's commitment to sustainability creates wide-reaching effects that influence behaviors across industries and even consumers' personal habits.

Case Study: Patagonia's Transparent Supply Chain Initiatives

Patagonia's commitment to environmental and social responsibility highlights the ripple effect of ethical decision-making. By publicly sharing details about its supply chain, including challenges like environmental impact and fair labor practices, Patagonia invites customers and partners to engage in its mission of sustainable sourcing. This transparency has led other companies to adopt similar practices, amplifying Patagonia's influence on industry standards for ethical sourcing.

Patagonia's transparency fosters trust with consumers and has inspired a broader movement toward responsible manufacturing in the apparel industry. This case demonstrates how an organization's ethical decisions can have far-reaching effects, influencing industry practices and customer expectations.

Managing Ripple Effects in Real Time

- **Rapid Response to Emerging Consequences**: Sometimes ripple effects reveal themselves in real time. Leaders can cultivate agility by being prepared to adjust and respond to new information.

- **Communicating the Why Behind Decisions**: To manage ripple effects on morale and trust, leaders can explain the reasoning and broader context of their decisions, promoting transparency and understanding.

- **Encouraging Employee Feedback**: By fostering open channels of communication, leaders can stay attuned to the effects of their decisions and respond swiftly if adjustments are needed.

Reflection and Action Points

- How can you incorporate a "ripple effect" mindset in your decision-making process?

- What potential secondary effects do you anticipate from recent or upcoming decisions?

- In what ways can you foster open communication to understand how decisions affect different parts of the organization?

Embracing the ripple effect of decisions helps leaders to cultivate awareness, accountability, and compassion. With this perspective, leaders move beyond isolated decision-making, creating choices that align with the values of the organization and positively influence the systems they serve.

Closing Thoughts on Part 3: Leading Through Systems Awareness

Systems thinking offers leaders a powerful tool to understand, navigate, and enhance organizational ecosystems. By embracing the complexity of interconnectedness, they can create positive ripple effects and build adaptable, resilient organizations that are capable of thriving in an ever-evolving world. Through the integration of systems thinking, leaders step into their roles not just as managers, but as stewards of a larger purpose.

Part 4:

Transformational Empowerment

Enabling Purposeful Action

Chapter 7:
Cultivating Self-Awareness and Autonomy

"Empowerment begins with self-awareness, enabling leaders and teams to align personal values with purposeful action."

True empowerment goes beyond delegation; it is rooted in self-awareness and autonomy. Transformational empowerment encourages leaders to foster environments where team members can discover their unique strengths, values, and goals—and where they are trusted to act on them. In this chapter, we explore how leaders can cultivate self-awareness, both within themselves and among their teams, to enable a greater sense of purpose and autonomy.

Why Self-Awareness is Essential for Empowerment

- **Aligning Actions with Values**: Leaders who cultivate self-awareness gain clarity on their own values and goals. When these values are shared openly, they can inspire and guide team actions in ways that resonate with shared purpose.

- **Recognizing Strengths and Growth Areas**: Self-awareness helps leaders and team members identify both their strengths and areas for development, creating a foundation for effective empowerment.

- **Encouraging Authenticity and Engagement**: When individuals understand and embrace their authentic selves, they are more likely to engage fully and bring creativity, resilience, and passion to their work.

Developing Self-Awareness as a Leader

1. **Reflection Practices**: Leaders can benefit from journaling, meditation, or regular reflection exercises that help them connect with their inner motivations and values.

2. **Seeking Feedback**: Honest feedback from peers, mentors, or coaches can reveal blind spots and offer valuable insights into personal growth areas.

3. **Mindfulness in Action**: Practicing mindfulness helps leaders stay present, manage stress, and make conscious choices aligned with their core values.

Fostering Self-Awareness and Autonomy in Teams

- **Personal Vision Statements**: Encourage team members to articulate their personal values and goals. This exercise fosters autonomy, helping them align their purpose with the organization's mission.

- **Strength-Based Development**: Help team members identify their unique strengths and how they can leverage them in their roles, empowering them to take ownership of their growth.

- **Decision-Making Autonomy**: Allow team members greater decision-making freedom within their roles, building trust and encouraging a proactive approach to problem-solving.

Real-World Applications of Self-Awareness and Autonomy

- **Case Study of Empowered Teams**: Examples of organizations that cultivate self-awareness and autonomy within their teams, leading to higher engagement, satisfaction, and innovation.

- **Leaders as Models of Self-Awareness**: Highlight leaders who exemplify self-awareness, showing how they inspire others to find and act on their authentic strengths.

Example: Zappos' Holacracy Model for Employee Empowerment

Zappos adopted a "holacracy" management model that replaces traditional hierarchy with self-managed teams. Employees are encouraged to take ownership of their roles, and job titles are removed to emphasize contribution over status. This approach promotes autonomy, giving team members a sense of purpose and accountability within the organization.

Case Study: Microsoft's Growth Mindset Culture Under Satya Nadella

When Satya Nadella became CEO of Microsoft, he introduced a growth mindset culture that emphasized learning over static goals. He encouraged employees to develop self-awareness by recognizing their strengths and areas for improvement. Microsoft's transformation into a learning organization has contributed to greater autonomy, innovation, and collaboration, reflecting how self-awareness fuels personal and organizational growth.

Reflection and Action Points

- How well do your personal values align with your actions and decisions as a leader?
- In what ways can you encourage your team to explore and embrace their own values and strengths?

- How can you create a more autonomous work environment that empowers individuals to make meaningful contributions?

Cultivating self-awareness and autonomy within your team strengthens their connection to their work, builds trust, and creates a culture of empowerment. Through this process, individuals find not just a job, but a purpose, which energizes both personal and collective goals.

Chapter 8:
Coaching for Purpose and Potential

"A leader's greatest impact lies in inspiring others to unlock their own potential and realize a shared vision."

The shift from managing to coaching represents a fundamental change in leadership—one that focuses on developing people rather than directing them. Transformational empowerment encourages leaders to step into the role of coach, guiding their team members toward discovering purpose, cultivating skills, and unlocking potential. In this chapter, we explore coaching techniques that enable leaders to foster a culture of continuous growth and empowerment.

The Power of a Coaching Mindset

- **Fostering Growth Over Control**: A coaching mindset encourages leaders to see themselves as facilitators of growth rather than controllers of output. By prioritizing development, they create an environment where individuals are motivated to reach their full potential.

- **Helping People Discover Purpose**: Purpose-driven employees are naturally more engaged and committed. Coaching provides a structure for helping individuals connect their personal goals with the organization's mission.

- **Creating Accountability with Compassion**: Coaches foster accountability by setting clear goals and expectations, but they do so with compassion, understanding that each person has a unique journey and pacing.

Essential Coaching Skills for Leaders

1. **Active Listening**: Effective coaching starts with listening—deeply and without interruption. Leaders who listen actively create space for team members to express ideas, goals, and concerns openly.

2. **Asking Powerful Questions**: Great coaches don't provide answers; they ask questions that encourage reflection and problem-solving, helping team members find solutions within themselves.

3. **Setting Clear and Challenging Goals**: Coaching is goal-oriented, so setting clear, challenging, and achievable goals helps team members focus on their development while contributing to larger organizational goals.

Coaching Techniques for Empowering Potential

- **Individual Development Plans**: Work collaboratively with each team member to set personalized development goals that align with both their personal aspirations and organizational needs.

- **Strengths-Based Feedback**: Focus feedback on individuals' strengths, highlighting what they are doing well and encouraging them to build on these skills.

- **Regular Check-Ins and Progress Reviews**: Consistent one-on-one sessions provide opportunities to celebrate progress, identify challenges, and adjust goals as needed, fostering a continuous growth mindset.

Practical Case Studies in Leadership Coaching

- **Example of a Leader-Driven Coaching Culture**: An in-depth look at an organization that has successfully embraced a coaching culture, resulting in high employee satisfaction, productivity, and innovation.

- **Leaders as Coaches and Mentors**: Profiles of leaders who serve as coaches, demonstrating how this approach has empowered team members to reach new heights in their careers and lives.

Example: LEGO's Agile Product Development for Sustainability

LEGO's commitment to sustainability led it to invest in finding eco-friendly materials to replace traditional plastic bricks. Recognizing the complexity and uncertainty of the transition, LEGO adopted an agile development process. The company continuously tests plant-based plastics and biodegradable materials, collecting feedback from customers to refine its approach.

LEGO's iterative, feedback-driven process enables it to pivot quickly in response to new research and customer input, embodying the agility needed to address environmental challenges. This example demonstrates how agile leadership supports sustainable innovation, even in the face of ongoing unknowns.

Case Study: Airbnb's Adaptation During the COVID-19 Pandemic

When COVID-19 drastically reduced global travel, Airbnb's core business model was threatened. To adapt, Airbnb swiftly pivoted by creating *Airbnb Experiences*, a new product that offered online experiences such as virtual cooking classes and guided city tours. This agile move allowed Airbnb to continue generating revenue and engage with users, despite restrictions on travel.

Airbnb's quick response to the unknown challenges of the pandemic demonstrated its agility and willingness to adapt. By creating a new revenue stream through virtual experiences, Airbnb not only sustained its business but also set an example of resilience and creativity in a time of crisis.

Reflection and Action Points

- How can you transition from a directive approach to a coaching mindset with your team?
- What powerful questions can you incorporate into your coaching conversations?
- In what ways can you help your team members set and achieve personal and professional development goals?

By embracing a coaching approach, leaders can help individuals unlock their potential, find purpose in their work, and take ownership of their development journey. Coaching for purpose and potential is more than a managerial technique; it is a path to empowering people to discover and bring forth their best selves.

Closing Thoughts on Part 4: Embracing Transformational Empowerment

Transformational empowerment combines self-awareness with purpose-driven coaching, creating a work environment where individuals feel seen, valued, and encouraged to grow. When leaders cultivate self-awareness and autonomy, they unlock the potential of every team member, building a collective foundation for success that transcends individual contributions. Through coaching and empowerment, leaders elevate their teams from followers to co-creators, each with a unique purpose aligned with a shared mission.

Part 5:

Distributed and Inclusive Leadership

Sharing Power

Chapter 9:
Distributed Decision-Making

"True empowerment means sharing the decision-making process, allowing team members to lead from where they are."

Distributed decision-making shifts the authority and responsibility from a few individuals at the top to empowered team members throughout the organization. This approach fosters agility, increases morale, and builds a culture where leadership is shared rather than centralized. In this chapter, we'll examine how distributed decision-making works in practice and how leaders can foster a culture that trusts and empowers people to make impactful decisions at all levels.

What is Distributed Decision-Making?

- **Moving Beyond Hierarchy**: Unlike traditional top-down decision-making, distributed decision-making empowers individuals to act with autonomy and confidence within their roles.

- **Trust as a Foundation**: A distributed model requires trust and transparency, where team members feel they have both the information and the authority to make informed decisions.

- **Improving Agility and Innovation**: By reducing bottlenecks, distributed decision-making enables faster responses to challenges, encourages innovation, and strengthens problem-solving skills across the organization.

Benefits of a Distributed Decision-Making Culture

- **Enhanced Ownership and Accountability**: When people are involved in decision-making, they take greater ownership and feel more accountable for outcomes, resulting in stronger engagement and commitment.

- **Greater Adaptability to Change**: Distributed decision-making empowers organizations to respond quickly to dynamic environments, as decisions don't require prolonged approval processes.

- **Empowering Innovation from All Levels**: Leaders are often amazed by the creativity and ingenuity that emerge when team members are free to make decisions, experiment, and innovate.

Steps to Cultivate Distributed Decision-Making

1. **Define Clear Boundaries and Autonomy**: Identify which decisions can be made at different levels within the organization, ensuring that team members understand their scope and authority.

2. **Provide Access to Information**: Empowering decision-making requires transparency. Leaders should ensure that team members have the data, resources, and context needed to make informed choices.

3. **Encourage Cross-Functional Collaboration**: In a distributed model, decisions often span multiple departments. Leaders can foster collaboration by creating structures where cross-functional teams can work together seamlessly.

Case Studies of Distributed Decision-Making in Action

- **Example of an Organization That Thrives on Autonomy**: Stories of companies that operate successfully with distributed decision-making, illustrating how it fosters resilience and innovation.

- **Leaders Who Champion Shared Power**: Profiles of leaders who prioritize distributed leadership, demonstrating the positive impact on team morale, accountability, and performance.

Example: Spotify's Squad Model for Distributed Leadership

Spotify's "squad" model organizes teams into small, autonomous groups that are responsible for their own areas of product development. Each squad operates like a small startup within the larger organization, with the flexibility to make decisions independently. This distributed leadership structure enhances adaptability and allows Spotify to respond quickly to market changes.

Case Study: The Morning Star Company's Self-Management System

The Morning Star Company, a tomato processing business, operates on a self-management system where employees are empowered to make their own decisions. Each person drafts a "Colleague Letter of Understanding" that details their responsibilities and commitments, fostering a sense of ownership and accountability. This distributed model has enabled Morning Star to thrive as one of the largest tomato processors, illustrating the power of distributed decision-making.

Reflection and Action Points

- How can you start to shift decision-making authority to empower others within your team?
- In what ways can you increase transparency and provide the information your team needs to make sound decisions?

- What are potential barriers to distributed decision-making in your organization, and how might you address them?

Distributed decision-making encourages a shared sense of responsibility and fosters an environment where team members are empowered to lead from within. By embracing this approach, leaders build an organization that thrives on collaboration, trust, and adaptability.

Chapter 10:
Embracing Diversity, Equity, and Inclusion

"A truly inclusive leader values diverse voices, fostering a culture where everyone is heard, valued, and empowered to contribute."

Inclusive leadership extends beyond traditional diversity initiatives by weaving equity and inclusion into the fabric of everyday interactions. Leaders who prioritize diversity, equity, and inclusion (DEI) embrace the perspectives, talents, and experiences that each team member brings, creating an environment where people feel they belong and are encouraged to succeed. In this chapter, we explore the principles and practices of inclusive leadership, highlighting how it contributes to greater organizational strength, creativity, and resilience.

The Principles of Inclusive Leadership

- **Valuing Diverse Perspectives**: Inclusive leaders recognize that diversity enriches discussions, drives innovation, and leads to better decision-making by bringing varied viewpoints to the table.

- **Creating Psychological Safety**: Inclusive environments are places where individuals feel safe to express themselves without fear of judgment or repercussion, knowing their unique perspectives are valued.

- **Commitment to Equity**: Leaders focus on equity by providing the support, opportunities, and resources that each team member needs to succeed, addressing systemic barriers and fostering a fair environment.

Building an Inclusive Culture

1. **Recruit and Retain Diverse Talent**: Building an inclusive organization starts with diverse hiring practices that ensure all voices and backgrounds are represented and respected.

2. **Encourage Open Dialogue and Feedback**: Leaders should foster open discussions about inclusion, inviting feedback on policies and practices and actively listening to team members' experiences.

3. **Challenge Unconscious Bias**: Through awareness training and regular self-reflection, leaders can identify and address biases that may unconsciously impact decision-making and workplace dynamics.

Practices for Inclusive Leadership

- **Inclusive Meetings**: Inclusive leaders ensure that all voices are heard, actively encouraging contributions from everyone and avoiding domination by a few. Techniques like round-robin sharing or anonymous input tools can help achieve this.

- **Mentorship and Sponsorship Programs**: Leaders can promote inclusivity by supporting mentorship programs that help underrepresented team members develop skills, build networks, and advance within the organization.

- **Establishing Clear Pathways for Advancement**: Inclusive leaders work to create transparent advancement opportunities, ensuring that all team members have the chance to progress based on their contributions and abilities.

Real-World Examples of Inclusive Leadership

- **Case Studies of Organizations Leading in DEI**: Stories of companies that have successfully embedded diversity, equity, and inclusion into their culture, demonstrating the tangible benefits of inclusive leadership.

- **Leaders who Model Inclusion and Equity**: Profiles of leaders who are DEI champions, showing how their commitment to inclusivity strengthens team cohesion, trust, and performance.

Example: Google's "Project Aristotle" for Team Inclusivity

Google's Project Aristotle studied the dynamics of successful teams, finding that psychological safety—where members feel safe to speak up without fear—was a key factor in high performance. Google implemented practices to create inclusive environments where team members could express themselves openly, reinforcing the importance of inclusion in collaborative success.

Case Study: Salesforce's Commitment to Workplace Equality

Salesforce has committed to equity through transparent tracking and closing of pay gaps. The company's CEO, Marc Benioff, champions equality by publicly advocating for DEI initiatives and implementing policies that ensure pay equity across gender and ethnicity. Salesforce's success in this area demonstrates the importance of accountability and transparency in DEI leadership.

Reflection and Action Points

- How can you identify and address barriers to diversity, equity, and inclusion within your organization?
- In what ways can you foster open dialogue and encourage feedback on DEI efforts?

- What steps can you take to become more aware of your own biases and work toward a more inclusive approach?

Embracing diversity, equity, and inclusion requires a dedicated and consistent effort. Inclusive leaders not only see the value of diversity but actively create pathways for all team members to thrive, transforming the workplace into an environment of belonging and shared growth.

Closing Thoughts on Part 5: Leading Through Shared Power and Inclusion

Distributed and inclusive leadership is about more than simply empowering individuals; it's about building an organization where everyone feels their contributions are valued and impactful. By fostering distributed decision-making and prioritizing inclusivity, leaders create a culture that respects diverse perspectives, empowers every team member, and strengthens the organization from within. These qualities are essential for building resilient, adaptive, and purpose-driven teams that can navigate a rapidly changing world with compassion and cohesion.

Part 6:

Mindful Leadership

Leading with Presence and Compassion

Chapter 11:
The Practice of Mindfulness in Leadership

"Mindful leadership begins with presence—the ability to be fully engaged in the moment, creating space for clarity, resilience, and authentic connection."

In today's fast-paced, high-stress work environments, mindfulness offers leaders a way to slow down, become more intentional, and develop a sense of inner calm and clarity. Mindfulness is not only a personal practice but a powerful leadership tool that enhances focus, reduces stress, and fosters better decision-making. In this chapter, we delve into the fundamentals of mindful leadership, exploring how leaders can cultivate a mindfulness practice to improve their well-being and elevate their influence.

What is Mindfulness in Leadership?

- **Presence and Awareness**: Mindfulness is the art of being fully present and aware without judgment. Leaders who practice mindfulness develop heightened focus, allowing them to be more attentive to people, situations, and opportunities.

- **Emotional Balance**: Mindfulness cultivates emotional intelligence, helping leaders manage stress, respond with composure, and build resilience in challenging situations.

- **Intentionality and Clarity**: Mindful leaders make decisions with greater clarity, engaging thoughtfully with both immediate tasks and long-term goals.

Benefits of Mindful Leadership

- **Enhanced Decision-Making**: Leaders who practice mindfulness are better equipped to approach decisions with a calm, clear mind, which can reduce impulsive reactions and increase strategic foresight.

- **Improved Relationships and Communication**: Mindful presence helps leaders communicate more effectively, listen deeply, and build stronger connections with team members.

- **Increased Resilience and Well-Being**: Mindfulness reduces stress and improves overall well-being, enabling leaders to stay grounded, focused, and resilient in the face of adversity.

Developing a Mindfulness Practice

1. **Start with Small, Consistent Practices**: Leaders new to mindfulness can begin with a few minutes of daily meditation or breathing exercises, gradually building their practice over time.

2. **Practice Presence in Daily Interactions**: Cultivate mindfulness in everyday interactions by practicing active listening, maintaining eye contact, and being fully present with colleagues.

3. **Engage in Reflection**: Daily or weekly reflection helps leaders assess how their mindfulness practice is impacting their leadership style, relationships, and decision-making.

Case Studies on Mindful Leadership in Action

- **Mindful Leaders in High-Pressure Environments**: Stories of leaders who have incorporated mindfulness to manage stress, boost team morale, and lead more effectively.
- **Organizations that Embrace Mindful Leadership**: Profiles of companies that prioritize mindfulness practices and the positive impact this has on employee well-being, engagement, and productivity.

Example: LinkedIn's Mindfulness Program

LinkedIn provides meditation and mindfulness training for employees, supported by onsite quiet rooms and mindfulness sessions. These practices help LinkedIn's workforce manage stress and enhance focus, contributing to a positive, supportive work environment.

Case Study: Aetna's Corporate Mindfulness Program

Under former CEO Mark Bertolini, Aetna introduced a mindfulness and yoga program to support employee well-being. The program reduced stress and increased productivity, with participating employees reporting higher job satisfaction. Aetna's investment in mindfulness demonstrates how mindful practices can benefit both individuals and the organization.

Reflection and Action Points

- What small steps can you take to incorporate mindfulness into your daily routine?
- How might mindfulness help you approach decisions and challenges more thoughtfully?

- In what ways can you practice being fully present with your team members?

Mindful leadership is about creating the mental space to be fully engaged, aware, and compassionate. By embracing mindfulness, leaders become more resilient, balanced, and intentional, qualities that ripple out to their teams and organizations.

Chapter 12:
Leadership in Action

"Compassionate leadership is the practice of leading with empathy, kindness, and a genuine commitment to the well-being of others."

While mindfulness focuses on inner awareness, compassionate leadership extends this awareness outward, nurturing empathy and understanding toward others. Compassionate leaders create environments where people feel valued, respected, and motivated to contribute their best. In this chapter, we explore how compassionate leadership transforms workplace culture, enhances employee engagement, and builds strong, trust-based relationships.

The Core Elements of Compassionate Leadership

- **Empathy and Understanding**: Compassionate leaders prioritize understanding others' perspectives and emotional experiences, fostering an environment of psychological safety and trust.

- **Authentic Kindness**: Compassionate leadership is rooted in authentic kindness, treating others with respect and consideration even in challenging situations.

- **Commitment to Well-Being**: Compassionate leaders are genuinely invested in the well-being of their team members, understanding that people who feel supported are more likely to be engaged, productive, and resilient.

Building a Compassionate Leadership Style

1. **Practice Active Listening**: Compassionate leaders listen deeply, without interrupting or judging, to understand the needs, concerns, and aspirations of their team members.

2. **Respond with Patience and Support**: Leaders who respond with patience and support foster a culture where people feel safe to express their ideas, concerns, and challenges.

3. **Encourage Self-Compassion**: Leaders can model self-compassion, acknowledging their own challenges and treating themselves with kindness. This empowers others to do the same, creating a supportive and understanding team environment.

The Positive Impact of Compassionate Leadership

- **Increased Employee Engagement and Loyalty**: Compassionate leaders create workplaces where people feel seen and appreciated, leading to higher levels of engagement and loyalty.

- **Strengthened Team Dynamics**: Compassion builds trust, reduces conflicts, and fosters stronger collaboration, resulting in more effective and cohesive teams.

- **Enhanced Organizational Resilience**: Compassionate leaders help build resilient organizations by supporting team members through challenges, promoting mental well-being, and fostering a sense of community.

Examples of Compassionate Leadership in the Real World

- **Case Studies of Compassionate Leaders**: Stories of leaders who prioritize compassion, showing the positive impact on their teams, workplace culture, and organizational performance.
- **Organizations that Embed Compassion in Culture**: Examples of companies with policies and practices that reflect a commitment to compassion, from wellness programs to supportive work environments.

Example: Microsoft's Support for Mental Health

Microsoft actively promotes mental health awareness and resources, including access to counseling and stress management training. This emphasis on compassion demonstrates Microsoft's commitment to employee well-being, creating a culture of care and resilience.

Case Study: Marriott International's "Take Care" Program

Marriott's "Take Care" program prioritizes employee well-being, offering wellness benefits and mental health resources. The program reflects Marriott's commitment to compassion, helping employees feel valued and supported. This compassionate approach has strengthened Marriott's culture and increased employee loyalty.

Reflection and Action Points

- How can you incorporate more empathy and compassion into your daily interactions as a leader?
- What steps can you take to support the well-being of your team members more actively?
- In what ways can you encourage a culture of kindness and understanding within your organization?

Compassionate leadership goes beyond management; it creates a culture of care and mutual respect. By leading with compassion, leaders empower their teams, build stronger relationships, and create an environment where people feel genuinely valued and inspired to do their best.

Closing Thoughts on Part 6: Embracing Mindful and Compassionate Leadership

Mindful and compassionate leadership transforms not only leaders but the entire workplace. By fostering presence, empathy, and a genuine commitment to well-being, leaders become powerful forces for positive change. In this way, mindful and compassionate leadership builds resilient organizations, empowering people to work with purpose, creativity, and mutual respect. As leaders embrace these qualities, they model a path forward for their teams, one where work becomes a shared journey of growth and understanding.

Part 7:

Purpose-Driven Leadership

Guiding with Meaning

Chapter 13:
Discovering Organizational Purpose

"Purpose-driven leadership begins with clarity—a clear sense of why the organization exists and how it seeks to positively impact the world."

Purpose-driven organizations are built on a foundation of meaning and intention, where the mission goes beyond profit to create a positive impact for employees, customers, and communities. Leaders who cultivate a clear sense of organizational purpose inspire their teams to connect with a larger mission, building a culture where everyone feels motivated by shared values and goals. In this chapter, we explore how leaders can define, communicate, and embody an authentic purpose that aligns with their organization's vision and values.

The Importance of Purpose in Leadership

- **Inspiring Commitment and Engagement**: A well-defined purpose motivates employees by showing them how their work contributes to a larger cause, inspiring greater dedication and satisfaction.

- **Attracting and Retaining Talent**: Purpose-driven organizations attract individuals who are motivated by meaning, making it easier to recruit and retain talented people who align with the mission.

- **Building Resilience and Adaptability**: A strong purpose provides a guiding compass, enabling the organization to stay resilient in times of change and navigate challenges with clarity.

Defining an Authentic Organizational Purpose

1. **Reflect on Core Values and Vision**: Leaders should start by examining the organization's core values and vision, identifying the unique ways it can contribute positively to the world.

2. **Involve Stakeholders in the Process**: Purpose isn't just created at the top; involving employees, customers, and even community members can help shape a purpose that resonates broadly and genuinely reflects the organization's impact.

3. **Make Purpose Actionable**: Purpose must be more than an idea—it should translate into tangible actions, influencing day-to-day decisions, strategic planning, and employee engagement.

Embedding Purpose into the Organizational Culture

- **Communicate Purpose Consistently**: Leaders can reinforce the organization's purpose by communicating it consistently, linking it to daily operations and long-term goals.

- **Celebrate Purpose-Driven Successes**: Recognize and celebrate when the organization achieves milestones or makes a positive impact in alignment with its purpose, reinforcing the value of purpose-driven work.

- **Align Policies and Practices with Purpose**: Ensure that hiring practices, employee development, and corporate social responsibility initiatives are all in harmony with the organization's mission and values.

Case Studies of Purpose-Driven Organizations

- **Examples of Companies with Clear Missions**: Stories of organizations that have successfully defined and embedded their purpose, highlighting the positive impact on employee morale, customer loyalty, and brand reputation.
- **Leaders as Purpose Champions**: Profiles of leaders who champion purpose-driven initiatives, illustrating how they inspire their teams and contribute to a culture of meaningful work.

Example: Ben & Jerry's Social Mission

Ben & Jerry's promotes social and environmental justice as part of its purpose. The company integrates activism into its operations, championing causes like climate action and racial equality. This alignment of business with purpose drives loyalty among consumers who share the company's values.

Case Study: Unilever's Sustainable Living Plan

Unilever's Sustainable Living Plan integrates purpose into its business strategy, aiming to reduce environmental impact while improving health and well-being. This purpose-driven mission has attracted conscious consumers and motivated employees, underscoring how purpose strengthens brand and culture.

Reflection and Action Points

- How clearly defined is your organization's purpose, and does it resonate with your team?
- In what ways can you communicate and integrate this purpose more effectively into everyday operations?

- How can you ensure that purpose-driven goals are part of your strategic planning?

Discovering and embedding organizational purpose provides the clarity and motivation that inspire individuals to contribute their best. By leading with purpose, leaders can create a culture where everyone is aligned toward making a meaningful impact.

Chapter 14:
Inspiring Others with a Purpose-Driven Mission

"The most effective leaders inspire others by embodying the purpose they promote, creating a ripple effect that energizes and mobilizes teams."

Purpose-driven leadership is not just about defining a mission; it's about living it every day. Leaders who embody the organization's purpose in their actions, decisions, and interactions inspire others to follow their example. By connecting team members to the mission, leaders help individuals see the value of their contributions and encourage them to engage with passion and enthusiasm. In this chapter, we explore how leaders can inspire purpose-driven action, creating a powerful, unified sense of mission.

The Power of Purposeful Inspiration

- **Leading by Example**: Purposeful inspiration begins with leaders who practice what they preach, demonstrating the organization's values through their actions and decisions.

- **Connecting Roles to the Bigger Picture**: Leaders can inspire by showing each team member how their unique role contributes to the organization's mission, helping them see the value of their work beyond immediate tasks.

- **Encouraging Individual Purpose**: Great leaders understand that purpose is both collective and individual. By helping team members connect their personal goals to the organization's mission, leaders create alignment and foster fulfillment.

Strategies for Inspiring Purpose-Driven Action

1. **Share Stories of Impact**: Stories of how the organization positively impacts customers, communities, or the environment make the mission more tangible and real, helping employees connect emotionally with the purpose.

2. **Encourage Team Participation in Purpose-Related Initiatives**: Involve employees in projects, initiatives, or volunteering efforts that align with the organization's mission, providing them with opportunities to engage directly in purpose-driven work.

3. **Foster a Culture of Recognition and Appreciation**: Recognize and celebrate individuals and teams who embody the organization's values and contribute to its mission, reinforcing a culture of purpose and pride.

Overcoming Challenges in Purpose-Driven Leadership

- **Balancing Purpose with Profit**: While purpose is central, organizations still need to balance it with financial goals. Leaders must find ways to align profitability with purpose-driven initiatives, ensuring both remain sustainable.

- **Maintaining Authenticity**: Purpose-driven leadership requires consistency. Leaders must be transparent and authentic in how they communicate and act, or they risk eroding trust within the team.

- **Preventing Purpose Burnout**: Purpose can be a powerful motivator, but leaders must also support work-life balance and provide mental health resources to prevent burnout among team members passionate about the mission.

Examples of Leaders Inspiring Purpose-Driven Teams

- **Case Studies of Inspirational Leaders**: Stories of leaders who have successfully inspired their teams by embodying and communicating their purpose, illustrating the transformative power of purpose-driven leadership.

- **Purpose-Driven Success Stories**: Examples of purpose-led organizations achieving remarkable outcomes in innovation, employee engagement, and social impact through committed and inspired leadership.

Example: Tesla's Mission to Accelerate Sustainable Energy

Tesla's mission is to accelerate the world's transition to sustainable energy. This mission guides Tesla's product development, from electric vehicles to solar energy products and energy storage systems. Tesla's commitment to sustainability has inspired employees, partners, and customers to support a future powered by clean energy, creating a strong alignment between the company's goals and its stakeholders' values.

Tesla's purpose-driven mission has motivated other automotive and energy companies to invest in sustainable technology, demonstrating how a clear and ambitious mission can influence an entire industry and inspire others to contribute to global goals.

Case Study: TOMS Shoes and the "One for One" Model

TOMS Shoes, founded by Blake Mycoskie, introduced the "One for One" model, where each pair of shoes purchased meant a new pair donated to a child in need. This purpose-driven mission attracted socially conscious customers and created a community around TOMS's mission to improve lives through business. By clearly embodying its values, TOMS not only inspired customers but also mobilized employees, suppliers, and partners to contribute to its philanthropic goals.

This purpose-centered approach transformed TOMS into more than a brand; it became a movement. The "One for One" model has since inspired other companies to adopt similar buy-one-give-one initiatives, showing the ripple effect of a well-defined and inspiring mission.

Reflection and Action Points

- How can you better embody and communicate your organization's purpose to inspire others?
- What actions can you take to help team members see the value of their roles in relation to the mission?
- How can you support team members in aligning their individual purposes with the organization's purpose?

Inspiring others with purpose-driven leadership is about more than motivation; it's about cultivating a sense of shared destiny. Leaders who embody and communicate their organization's mission build teams who are not just motivated by tasks, but driven by a collective vision that unites and empowers them.

Closing Thoughts on Part 7: Leading with Purpose and Meaning

Purpose-driven leadership brings clarity, direction, and meaning to the workplace. Leaders who define and embody a clear mission inspire others to engage fully, aligning their personal goals with the organization's larger purpose. Through purpose-driven leadership, organizations become not only successful but transformative, creating a lasting positive impact on employees, customers, and communities. As we lead with purpose, we find ourselves contributing to something bigger than ourselves, creating value that resonates far beyond the workplace.

Part 8:

Quantum Leadership

Embracing Uncertainty and Adaptability

Chapter 15:
Seeing the Big Picture in Quantum Leadership

"Quantum leadership embraces the complexity of interconnected systems, where every decision, action, and interaction creates new possibilities."

In the realm of quantum leadership, leaders go beyond linear thinking, recognizing that the modern workplace is more like a dynamic web of interconnected systems than a simple hierarchy. Quantum leadership invites leaders to see the big picture, understanding that their actions influence the organization in both direct and subtle ways. This chapter explores how quantum leadership encourages adaptability, flexibility, and open-mindedness, allowing leaders to create environments that are resilient, innovative, and responsive to change.

What is Quantum Leadership?

- **Beyond Traditional Models**: Quantum leadership shifts away from rigid structures and fixed processes, embracing a view that values flexibility and dynamic relationships within the organization.

- **Seeing Possibilities, Not Limitations**: Quantum leaders are open to potential, looking for possibilities in every interaction and understanding that seemingly small actions can create significant ripple effects.

- **Balancing Paradoxes and Polarities**: In quantum leadership, leaders hold space for paradoxes, understanding that complex situations often require holding opposing perspectives simultaneously—for instance, balancing innovation with stability or vision with practicality.

Principles of Quantum Leadership

- **Interconnectedness and Wholeness**: Recognizing that every part of the organization influences and is influenced by the whole, leaders view their role as part of an interconnected system where collaboration and alignment create resilience.

- **Adaptability as a Core Strength**: Quantum leaders embrace change, approaching it with an open mind and a willingness to adapt, which builds resilience and agility in the face of evolving challenges.

- **Empowering Emergent Outcomes**: Quantum leadership values emergent outcomes, where results and solutions unfold through dynamic interactions among team members rather than through rigid planning alone.

Practical Strategies for Embracing Quantum Leadership

1. **Practice Systems Thinking**: Embrace a mindset that considers the whole organization as an ecosystem, understanding how each decision and action has wider implications.

2. **Encourage Experimentation and Learning**: Foster a culture where team members feel safe to try new ideas, learn from mistakes, and iterate, building adaptability and innovation.

3. **Hold Space for Paradox**: Quantum leaders don't need to choose between two opposing ideas; instead, they can hold space for both, seeking balance and creative solutions.

Examples of Quantum Leadership in Action

- **Case Studies of Quantum Thinking Leaders**: Stories of leaders who adopt quantum principles, demonstrating how they create adaptable, agile organizations that thrive in complexity.

- **Organizations with Quantum Culture**: Profiles of companies that prioritize flexibility, emergent solutions, and adaptability, showing how quantum leadership benefits culture and productivity.

Example: Tesla's Integrated and Agile Approach to Innovation

Tesla's approach to innovation illustrates a quantum perspective, blending interconnectedness and adaptability across its operations. By integrating design, engineering, and production under one roof, Tesla can rapidly adapt and implement new technologies, such as battery advancements and software updates. This agile model allows Tesla to pivot quickly in response to market trends, embodying the flexibility and interconnected thinking characteristic of quantum leadership.

Case Study: Haier's Decentralized Ecosystem of Micro-Enterprises

Chinese appliance giant Haier adopted a radical decentralized model, transforming its structure into an ecosystem of over 4,000 self-managed micro-enterprises. Each micro-enterprise operates independently, with freedom to innovate and respond quickly to market changes. This model embodies quantum leadership by allowing interconnected yet autonomous units to drive innovation. Haier's approach shows how embracing complexity and decentralization fosters resilience and adaptability in a global business environment.

Reflection and Action Points

- How can you expand your view of your organization as an interconnected system?

- What small experiments can you introduce to encourage learning and adaptability within your team?

- In what ways can you hold space for paradoxes, embracing complexity and ambiguity in your decisions?

Quantum leadership invites leaders to step back, see the bigger picture, and embrace a mindset of potential and adaptability. By practicing systems thinking and empowering emergent solutions, leaders help create environments where innovation and resilience naturally arise.

Chapter 16:
Leading with Agility and Embracing the Unknown

"To lead with agility is to see the unknown as a realm of possibilities, where adaptability and creativity turn uncertainty into opportunity."

Uncertainty can be daunting, but quantum leaders view it as an opportunity for growth, innovation, and transformation. Agile leadership goes hand-in-hand with quantum thinking, as both prioritize responsiveness, flexibility, and a willingness to adjust course as new information emerges. This chapter explores the principles of agile leadership within the quantum framework, helping leaders cultivate a mindset that thrives on change and turns the unknown into a source of strength.

The Foundations of Agility in Quantum Leadership

- **Embracing Change as a Constant**: Agile leaders understand that change is inevitable and continuous. They view it not as a disruption but as an essential part of growth and innovation.

- **Iterative Learning and Growth**: Agile leadership focuses on learning from each step, continuously iterating and improving processes, products, and approaches in real-time.

- **Encouraging Responsiveness**: Quantum leaders cultivate a culture where teams are ready to pivot, adjusting to evolving circumstances without losing sight of core values and goals.

Principles for Leading with Agility

1. **Value Adaptability Over Rigid Planning**: In agile leadership, flexibility is prioritized over strict adherence to long-term

plans, allowing leaders and teams to adjust quickly in response to changes.

2. **Focus on Incremental Progress**: Break down large projects into smaller, manageable steps, celebrating small wins and using feedback to inform next steps.

3. **Stay Open to Feedback and Evolution**: Agile leaders seek out feedback, viewing it as a valuable tool for continuous growth and alignment, both with team needs and organizational goals.

Building a Culture of Agility and Innovation

- **Empowering Teams with Decision-Making Freedom**: Agile leaders encourage distributed decision-making, empowering team members to make adjustments and take ownership of their tasks and projects.

- **Fostering a Growth Mindset**: By fostering a mindset that sees challenges as learning opportunities, leaders build resilience and optimism within the team, making them more adaptable to future changes.

- **Celebrating Flexibility and Learning**: Emphasize that success is not always about flawless execution but about the willingness to learn, adapt, and evolve.

Case Studies of Agile Leaders Embracing the Unknown

- **Examples of Leaders Adapting in Real Time**: Stories of leaders who have embraced agility, showing how they've successfully navigated uncertainty and turned challenges into opportunities for growth.

- **Organizations that Thrive on Agility**: Profiles of companies that excel in a fast-paced, uncertain environment by fostering an agile culture where experimentation, learning, and responsiveness are valued.

Example: Netflix's Data-Driven Agility in Content Creation

Netflix uses a data-driven approach to monitor viewing patterns and preferences, adapting content to suit audience demand in real time. This approach enabled Netflix to pioneer its shift to original programming, releasing series and films that resonate with viewers globally. Netflix's agility in responding to real-time data insights shows how leaders can embrace the unknown, using feedback loops to guide decision-making and innovation.

Case Study: Adobe's "Kickbox" Innovation Program

Adobe introduced its "Kickbox" program to empower employees at all levels to pursue innovative ideas. Each employee is given a "Kickbox" containing resources to explore and develop their concept autonomously. Adobe's approach allows employees to experiment without fear of failure, adapting to new ideas and trends with agility. The program exemplifies how agile, quantum leadership empowers teams to embrace the unknown, fostering a culture of learning and experimentation.

Reflection and Action Points

- What changes can you make to prioritize agility and responsiveness within your team?
- How can you encourage a culture that sees learning as an ongoing process rather than an end goal?

- In what ways can you support your team in embracing uncertainty and approaching challenges with a growth mindset?

Leading with agility and embracing the unknown allows quantum leaders to build organizations that are resilient, flexible, and prepared to navigate any challenge. By prioritizing adaptability and creating a culture that values learning and iteration, leaders turn uncertainty into a source of possibility and growth.

Closing Thoughts on Part 8: Navigating Complexity with Quantum and Agile Leadership

Quantum and agile leadership go hand-in-hand, guiding leaders through the complexities of today's dynamic environment with flexibility, openness, and responsiveness. By embracing a quantum mindset and fostering agility, leaders not only prepare themselves and their teams for the unknown but also cultivate a culture that thrives in it. This combination allows organizations to be nimble, innovative, and resilient, making quantum leadership a crucial approach for navigating the evolving landscape of modern business and society.

Part 9:

Resonant Leadership

Cultivating Emotional Connection

Chapter 17:
Building Trust Through Emotional Resonance

"Resonant leaders inspire trust by connecting emotionally with their teams, creating an environment where people feel safe, valued, and motivated to contribute."

Trust is at the core of effective leadership, and resonant leaders build trust by creating genuine emotional connections with their team members. Emotional resonance refers to a leader's ability to attune to the emotions, needs, and aspirations of others, fostering empathy and understanding. In this chapter, we explore how emotional resonance strengthens trust, boosts morale, and builds a resilient foundation for collaboration and growth.

What is Emotional Resonance in Leadership?

- **Connecting on a Human Level**: Emotional resonance is about creating meaningful connections beyond professional roles, showing empathy, and valuing individuals for who they are.

- **Promoting Psychological Safety**: Resonant leaders foster an environment where team members feel safe to voice ideas, take risks, and be themselves without fear of judgment.

- **Encouraging Emotional Transparency**: Leaders who model openness about their emotions encourage others to do the same, creating a culture where people feel understood and supported.

Why Trust is Essential in Resonant Leadership

- **Boosting Engagement and Motivation**: When people trust their leaders, they are more likely to engage deeply, feel committed to the mission, and go above and beyond in their roles.

- **Creating Cohesion and Reducing Turnover**: Trust fosters loyalty and cohesion within teams, leading to greater retention and a stronger sense of community.

- **Supporting Resilience in Times of Challenge**: Trust-based relationships create a resilient organizational culture, allowing teams to adapt and stay connected through times of uncertainty.

Steps to Build Trust through Emotional Resonance

1. **Practice Active Listening with Empathy**: Listening deeply to understand rather than respond is a cornerstone of emotional resonance. Leaders should make an effort to truly hear and validate team members' perspectives.

2. **Be Transparent and Authentic**: Trust thrives when leaders are open about their own experiences, challenges, and emotions, creating a safe space for others to be genuine as well.

3. **Recognize and Appreciate Contributions**: Show appreciation for team members' efforts and recognize their achievements. When people feel valued, trust naturally grows.

Real-World Examples of Trust-Building Leaders

- **Stories of Leaders Who Prioritize Trust**: Examples of leaders who actively build trust through emotional resonance, showing the positive impacts on team morale, productivity, and retention.

- **Organizations with Trust-Based Cultures**: Profiles of companies that emphasize trust and emotional resonance, demonstrating how this foundation supports resilience and collaboration.

Example: The Ritz-Carlton's "Gold Standards" of Service

The Ritz-Carlton's Gold Standards are a set of service principles that emphasize empathy, respect, and emotional connection. Employees are trained to "fulfill even the unexpressed wishes" of guests, fostering a culture of trust and emotional connection. By empowering employees to make decisions that enhance the guest experience, Ritz-Carlton demonstrates the value of trust and emotional resonance in delivering exceptional service.

Case Study: Howard Schultz's Emotional Connection at Starbucks

When Howard Schultz returned as CEO of Starbucks, he prioritized emotional connection by listening to employees and engaging them in shaping the company's direction. His personal outreach, like closing stores for employee training, underscored his commitment to a culture of trust and emotional resonance. This connection revitalized the Starbucks community, highlighting how emotional resonance builds trust and loyalty within teams.

Reflection and Action Points

- How can you improve your active listening skills to better connect with your team?
- In what ways can you model authenticity to create an emotionally safe workplace?
- What steps can you take to ensure team members feel recognized and valued?

Building trust through emotional resonance not only strengthens relationships but also builds a foundation of mutual respect and loyalty that supports an engaged, cohesive, and high-performing team.

Chapter 18:
Fostering a Positive Organizational Culture

"A resonant leader cultivates a positive culture where team members feel uplifted, empowered, and inspired to contribute their best."

Organizational culture shapes everything from employee morale to productivity and retention. Resonant leaders recognize the profound impact of a positive culture, prioritizing emotional well-being, collaboration, and mutual respect. In this chapter, we explore how leaders can foster an uplifting organizational culture that encourages personal growth, nurtures creativity, and brings out the best in each individual.

The Elements of a Positive Organizational Culture

- **Alignment with Shared Values**: A positive culture is rooted in shared values, where individuals feel connected to the mission and motivated by a sense of purpose.

- **Encouraging Personal and Professional Growth**: Leaders in positive cultures prioritize continuous learning, creating opportunities for team members to develop skills and achieve their goals.

- **Fostering Connection and Belonging**: When people feel they belong, they are more likely to collaborate openly, share ideas, and support one another, strengthening team dynamics and resilience.

Strategies for Creating a Positive Culture

1. **Establish Core Values and Communicate Them Regularly**: Clearly defining and reinforcing core values helps to align

team actions, decisions, and goals with the organization's mission, fostering a shared sense of purpose.

2. **Prioritize Well-Being and Work-Life Balance**: Leaders can create a positive culture by supporting well-being initiatives, encouraging breaks, and respecting boundaries, helping individuals maintain a healthy balance.

3. **Celebrate Successes and Learn from Challenges**: Recognizing achievements and openly discussing challenges creates a culture of growth and accountability, where team members feel empowered to learn from every experience.

Creating Opportunities for Connection and Engagement

- **Team-Building and Collaborative Initiatives**: Encourage regular team-building activities, retreats, or group projects to strengthen relationships and enhance collaboration.

- **Encouraging Open Dialogue and Feedback**: Leaders should create spaces where team members feel comfortable sharing feedback and discussing both successes and challenges, fostering transparency and continuous improvement.

- **Inclusive Celebrations and Recognition**: Recognize and celebrate diverse contributions, promoting a sense of inclusivity and shared accomplishment within the organization.

Case Studies of Positive Cultural Transformation

- **Examples of Organizations with Strong Cultures**: Stories of companies that have transformed their culture, highlighting the benefits of prioritizing positivity, collaboration, and personal growth.

- **Leaders Who Champion Positive Change**: Profiles of leaders who have successfully cultivated positive, resonant cultures, illustrating how this approach fosters innovation, resilience, and engagement.

Example: Southwest Airlines' Culture of Fun and Appreciation

Southwest Airlines cultivates a positive culture centered on humor, appreciation, and employee well-being. The airline encourages employees to engage with passengers in a warm, playful manner, creating memorable customer experiences. Southwest's focus on joy and community illustrates how a positive culture contributes to high employee morale, strong loyalty, and a resonant customer experience.

Case Study: Google's "Project Oxygen" for Employee Well-Being

Google's Project Oxygen identified key behaviors that make managers effective, such as empathy, empowerment, and active listening. By prioritizing these qualities, Google fosters a positive culture where employees feel valued and motivated. The project has led to increased employee satisfaction and retention, showing how resonant leadership principles can elevate organizational culture and improve well-being.

Reflection and Action Points

- How can you incorporate core values into everyday operations and decisions?
- What steps can you take to support well-being and work-life balance in your team?
- How can you create more opportunities for connection and recognition?

Fostering a positive organizational culture empowers individuals to feel connected, supported, and inspired. By prioritizing emotional well-being, alignment with values, and opportunities for growth, resonant leaders cultivate an environment where people are motivated to bring their best to the organization, collaborate with purpose, and contribute meaningfully to the collective mission.

Closing Thoughts on Part 9: Resonant Leadership – The Power of Emotional Connection and Positive Culture

Resonant leadership is the art of leading with heart—connecting deeply with people, building trust, and creating a positive environment where individuals feel valued, safe, and motivated. By fostering emotional resonance and cultivating a positive culture, leaders create teams that are not only productive but also resilient, innovative, and deeply engaged.

As we conclude this exploration of resonant leadership, it becomes clear that the most successful organizations are not merely collections of individuals working toward goals. Instead, they are communities united by shared purpose and mutual respect, where every member feels seen, heard, and appreciated. Resonant leaders recognize that their role is not only to lead but to uplift, inspire, and empower others.

In a world where change is constant, organizations with a foundation of trust and emotional connection are those best equipped to adapt, grow, and make a lasting positive impact. By embodying the principles of resonant leadership, you have the power to create an organization that thrives through collaboration, compassion, and shared purpose.

Conclusion: The Journey to Next-Level Leadership

Leadership today requires more than strategic thinking or management skills; it requires a commitment to growth, authenticity, and a genuine desire to make a difference. As we've explored across these chapters, next-level leadership draws on regenerative, mindful, inclusive, agile, and purpose-driven approaches to create workplaces that are resilient, innovative, and deeply connected.

This journey to next-level leadership is about embracing complexity, fostering connection, and leading with purpose and compassion. It is a call to action for leaders to become catalysts for positive change—not only within their organizations but in the world beyond.

As you move forward, remember that each step in your leadership journey is an opportunity to learn, grow, and inspire others. With every action, decision, and interaction, you have the power to create a legacy that uplifts, empowers, and contributes to a better, more conscious world.

Conclusion:
The Journey to Next-Level Leadership

"Leadership is not just a position; it's a purpose-driven journey that calls us to inspire, connect, and create positive change in every sphere we touch."

As we arrive at the end of this exploration, it's evident that next-level leadership transcends traditional boundaries and definitions. The modern leader is more than a strategist or a manager. They are a guide, a visionary, a source of inspiration, and a steward of collective well-being. This journey toward becoming a next-level leader is not a final destination, but an ongoing commitment to growth, adaptability, and conscious action.

Embracing a Holistic View of Leadership

Today's challenges require leaders who see the organization not just as a structure to manage, but as a living, interconnected ecosystem. Each part—each person, process, and purpose—interacts in a complex web of relationships and potential. Leaders who embrace systems thinking, who see the whole while respecting the unique contributions of each part, are the ones most equipped to create resilient and adaptable teams.

Integrating Purpose, Agility, and Emotional Connection

The chapters in this book have woven together elements of purpose-driven, mindful, and compassionate leadership, creating a mosaic of practices that support a more conscious approach to leading. Purpose-driven leaders align their teams with a mission that goes beyond profit, inspiring everyone to contribute their best to a shared vision. Agile leaders, embracing the unknown and adapting with resilience, empower their teams to pivot and innovate with confidence. And resonant leaders, fostering trust through emotional connection, create cultures where people feel valued, supported, and motivated to excel.

These principles work together to foster an organization that is not only successful but deeply connected to its people, its values, and its impact on the world.

Leaving a Legacy of Positive Impact

The true measure of leadership is not found solely in metrics or outcomes but in the positive ripple effects created within and beyond the organization. Next-level leaders inspire purpose and create environments where people can thrive. They leave a legacy of trust, compassion, and empowerment that goes beyond immediate achievements, shaping an enduring culture of well-being, innovation, and ethical responsibility.

In the end, next-level leadership is about contributing to a world where business becomes a force for good—a world where every action and decision honors the dignity of individuals and the sustainability of our shared environment.

The Ongoing Journey

Becoming a next-level leader is a journey, one that requires a commitment to continuous growth, reflection, and humility. As you lead, remember that each interaction is an opportunity to learn, adapt, and inspire others. Embrace the challenges that come, and see them as moments to grow stronger in your purpose and wiser in your decisions.

Let your journey be guided by empathy, curiosity, and a dedication to creating meaningful impact. Whether you are leading a team, an organization, or a community, your commitment to next-level leadership has the power to shape a future where people, planet, and purpose align harmoniously.

As you move forward, may you be empowered to lead with courage, connect with authenticity, and inspire others to rise with you in creating a more conscious, compassionate world.

About the Author

Zen Benefiel is a dynamic thought leader, author, and transformational coach dedicated to helping individuals and organizations unlock their highest potential through conscious leadership and purposeful action. With over three decades of experience in personal development, business consulting, and team dynamics, Zen has guided countless leaders and entrepreneurs on their journeys to create meaningful, impactful change in the world.

A passionate advocate for holistic approaches to leadership, Zen integrates principles from systems thinking, quantum theory, and regenerative practices into his work, empowering people to see the interconnectedness of their decisions and the ripple effects they create. A Royal Society for the Arts Fellow and rated a top Thought Leader for 2024 by Thinkers360.com, his work bridges the gap between traditional business practices and evolving paradigms of sustainability, emotional intelligence, and collective wisdom.

Zen holds multiple degrees in business, organizational management and transformational leadership and is a certified life coach and facilitator. He is also the Operations Director for the **Live and Let Live Foundation and Movement**, an organization dedicated to promoting freedom, peace, and ethical principles worldwide. In this role, Zen helps lead efforts to unite people across cultures and borders in the pursuit of a more harmonious and equitable world.

In addition, Zen is the founder of **Planetary Citizens**, a platform dedicated to global consciousness and collaborative leadership. Through his workshops, keynote speeches, and coaching sessions, Zen encourages leaders to embrace mindfulness, compassion, and co-creation as the cornerstones of a conscious leadership journey.

Beyond his professional endeavors, Zen is an avid golfer and drummer, finding balance and creativity through both activities. He also enjoys long hikes with his wife, Luba, where they explore nature together and reflect on life's deeper questions. A lifelong explorer of metaphysics, ancient wisdom traditions, and quantum realities, Zen seeks to align science and spirituality in the pursuit of personal and planetary harmony. His approach to leadership emphasizes both the practical and the profound, inspiring leaders to balance heart and mind, purpose and performance.

Zen Benefiel is the author of multiple books on personal growth, transformation, and leadership, including *"Stubbing My T.O.E. on Purpose"*, *"Awakening the Power Within"*, and *"The God Participle"*. Through his writings and teachings, Zen aims to catalyze a new wave of conscious leaders who are committed to service, sustainability, and creating a harmonious future for humanity and the planet.

When he's not guiding others on their leadership journeys, you can find Zen playing drums, improving his golf swing, or enjoying long hikes with Luba in the great outdoors, all while continuing his quest for deeper understanding and connection.

www.ingramcontent.com/pod-product-compliance
Lightning Source LLC
Chambersburg PA
CBHW050316230526
45471CB00005B/2209